A Sunshine Garden Doll Pattern

Primrose

By Anne Cote

Primrose

Daisy

For more Sunshine Garden Dolls Patterns
Visit bluedaisyzone.com

Sunflower

Poppy   **Dandelion**   **Marigold**   **Rosemary**   **Sage**   **Primrose**

ISBN-13: 978-1-940354-63-7

This book includes pattern templates that may be used for the original creation of the doll and any creative changes desired by the crafter. The templates themselves cannot be reproduced or sold in the original form.

Text, Photos, and Illustrations by Anne Cote
Cover Design by Anne Cote & Layne Walker
Edited by Joan Cote and Layne Walker

First edition published in August 2020
Published by New Friends Publishing, LLC
Lake Havasu City, AZ

Visit New Friends Publishing's Website at
www.newfriendspublishing.com

CONTENTS

To all my Dancer Friends,

who lift my heart

with

Love and Joy

Materials for Primrose

Primrose is a soft cuddly doll 20" tall with long yellow braids. She is dainty in her floral pastel dress and white

SUPPLIES

There are lots of options for materials, including scraps of fabric and fancy trims. I've listed the products I use in brackets. Other options abound and are listed below.

DOLL

44"x13" cotton fabric for body [Lightweight Muslin]
Craft paint, markers, pastel stick
    [Anita's Navy Blue for eyes; Anita's White for dots in the eyes]
    [Sharpie Permanent Markers for nose, brows, lashes, mouth]
    [Rosy pink pastel stick for cheeks]
Yarn for hair: yellow
Poly-fil Stuffing 6-8 oz.
Stuffing tools [tube and stick]
Fabric turning tools [tube and stick, see instructions]

CLOTHING

44"x19" cotton floral fabric for bloomers, top, and skirt
16"x7" eyelet fabric for apron skirt
32"x2" eyelet fabric for apron waist band & ties
20"x3" cotton fabric for hair bows
12"x8" black felt for shoes

30" 1/2"-1" lace trim (flat or gathered) for skirt
18" 1/2"-1" lace trim (flat or gathered) for bloomers
11" 1/2"-1" lace trim (flat or gathered) for neckline
11" 1/2"-1" lace trim (flat or gathered) for sleeves
    (Total trim: 70")
38"x1" gathered lace or eyelet for apron skirt and straps

18" 1/4" elastic for bloomers and skirt
2 snap fasteners
General sewing supplies

OPTIONS

Face can be painted, embroidered, or drawn on with permanent markers.
Cheek blush can be made with powdered blush or chalks.
Bloomers in a contrasting color takes 20"x10" of fabric.
Top in contrasting color takes 26"x7" of fabric.
Skirt in contrasting color takes 32x11" of fabric.
Hair instructions are for hand sewing. Glue can be used instead, or a combination of sewing and glue.
Hair Bow and/or Apron Waist Band & Ties can be made with bias tape or ribbon, rather than cut and sewn.
Trim can be flat or gathered.
Snaps can be plastic or metal or replaced by buttons.

COPYRIGHT and CHILD SAFETY

COPYRIGHT

What **CAN** you do? You **CAN** sell the items that you make from this pattern. You can use the templates to create the doll. You can also add your own artistic flare to what you create when using the templates. What you make is your property and is yours to do with as you wish.

What **CAN'T** you do? You **CANNOT** copy the pattern illustrations, diagrams, written instructions or photos. You cannot simply photocopy, scan, or reproduce the sewing pattern in any way and then sell copies of it. This is an infringement of copyright laws.

CHILD SAFETY

This doll is advised for children 3 years or older. For a younger child or baby, bows, sashes, ribbons, or any loose parts should be removed or sewn securely onto the doll or clothing. Fancy laces can wear out with use and separate from the clothing. They are preferable for children over 3. Plastic baby snaps can be used instead of metal snaps. The pattern calls for painting the face. Embroidery and painting are safety measures. Buttons should not be used for eyes for small children. I cannot be responsible for the way each crafter uses these patterns or instructions. Please consider the age of the child for which you are making the doll.

For more information on copyright laws and safety information, there is a great amount of information on the internet. For pattern questions, please send an email to Anne at this address: bluedaisyzone@gmail.com

Making the Doll

All seam allowances are 1/4 inch.

Use a small machine stich for more stability.

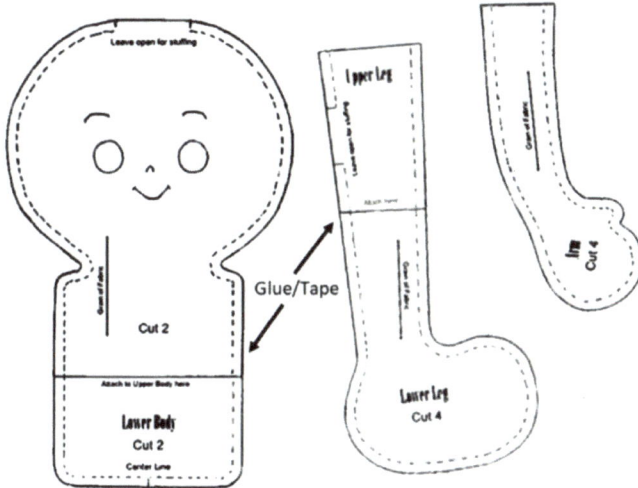

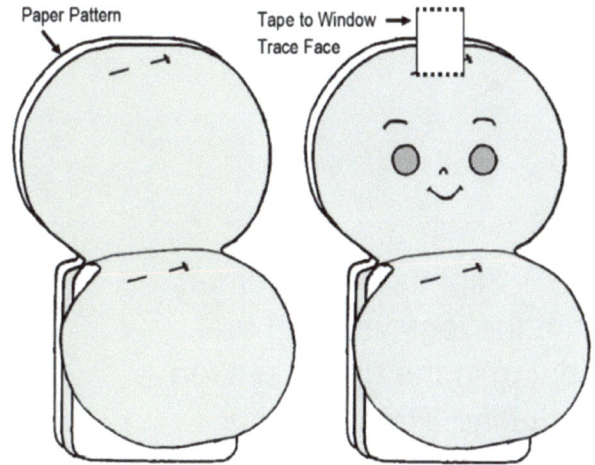

Cut out the patterns. Glue or tape the leg and body pieces together where indicated. Pin to fabric and cut out pieces.

FACE: Lay the fabric head/body on top of the paper pattern. Pin one side of the fabric head to the pattern top. Pin the folded layer of fabric to the lower body. Tape or hold the head/body to a window or lightbox and trace the face with pencil.

All the features can be painted or embroidered. I use acrylic paint for the eyes and Sharpie Permanent Markers for the nose, mouth, brows, and eyelashes. Don't forget to add a white dot to the eyes.

Primrose's eyes are bright blue. The lashes are black. The brows are brown. The nose and mouth are red. For her cheeks, a rosy pink powdered blush or pastel stick works well with her blue eyes and blond hair.

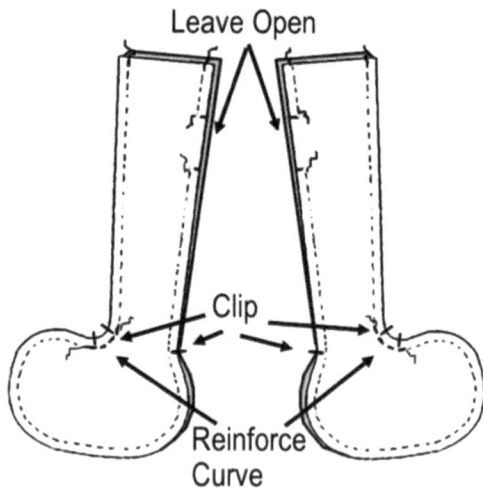

LEGS: Right sides together, stitch the legs, leaving the opening in the upper section for stuffing. Reinforce the curve between the top of the foot and leg. Clip curves.

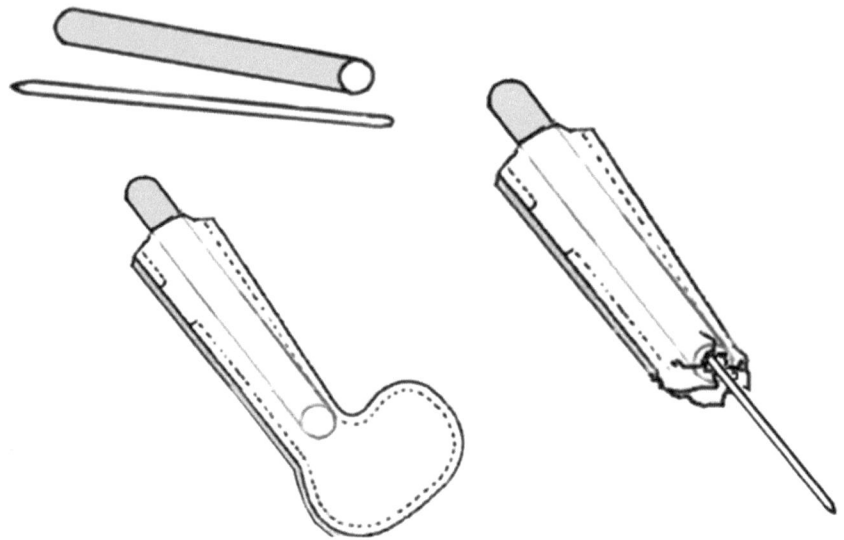

Turn the legs right side out. My favorite way of turning narrow fabric pieces is with a tube and stick. In this case, push the tube inside the leg. With the stick, push the foot into the tube until it comes out the other end.

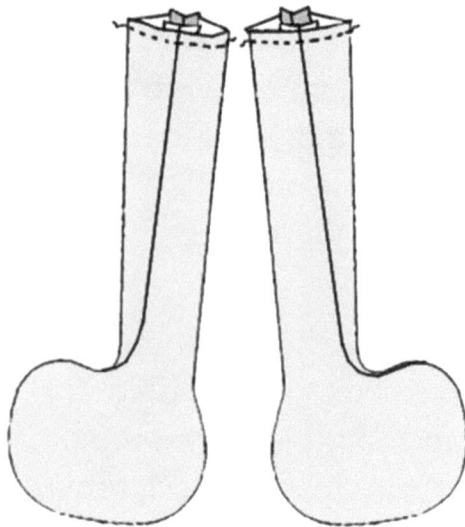

Open the top of the legs and pin the seams together. Baste across the top.

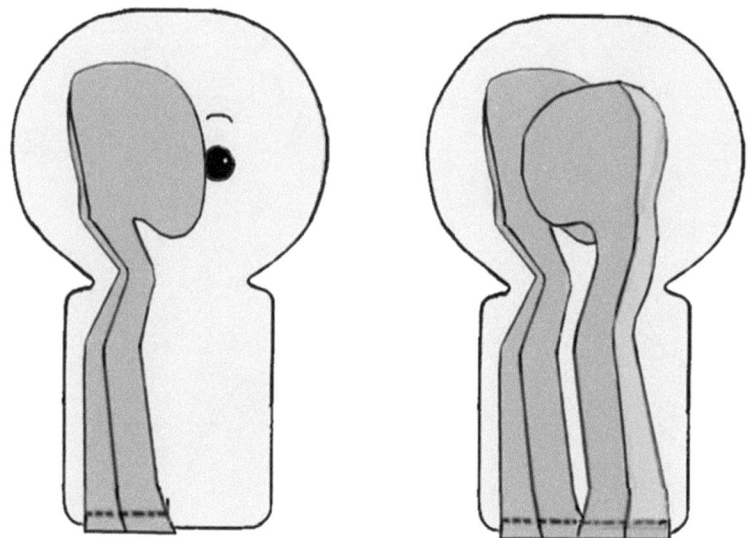

Place the top of the legs on the bottom of the right side of the body with the face. It's very important that the toes face the features on the face. Otherwise, the feet and legs will come out backwards. The leg tops should lie 1/4 inch from the side of the body on both sides. The legs should hang just below the body about 1/8 inch to make sure they are caught in the stitches. The legs might overlap a little in the middle. Pin/baste the legs in place along the bottom of the body.

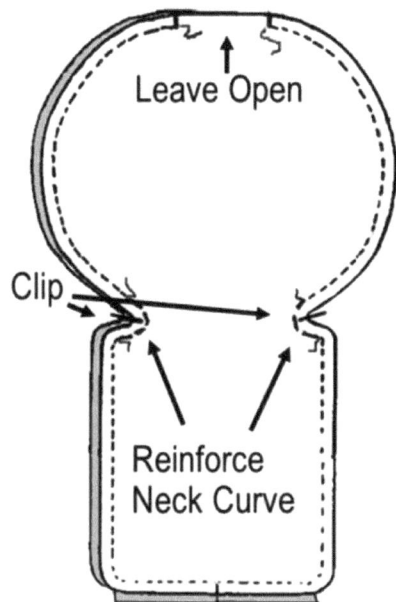

BODY: Right sides together, pin/baste the entire body, making sure the feet and legs are not caught in the seam allowance. Starting at the head, stitch around the entire body, leaving the opening for the stuffing. Reinforce the neck area with extra stitches. Clip the curves.

Turn the body right side out. Stuff the body and head. Sew the head closed with a ladder stitch as shown above.

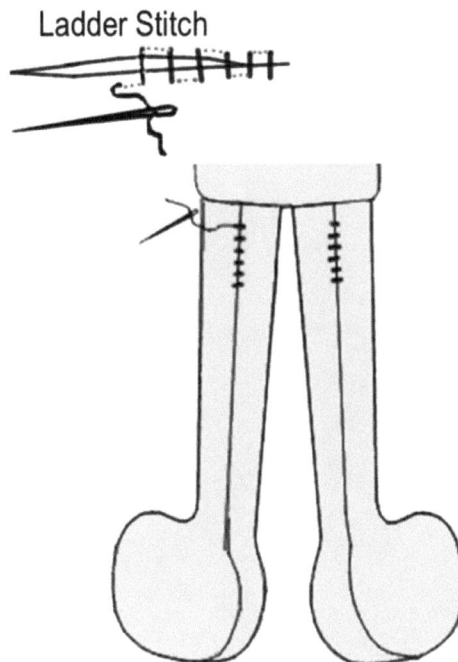

On the back side, stuff the legs. Close the legs with a ladder stitch.

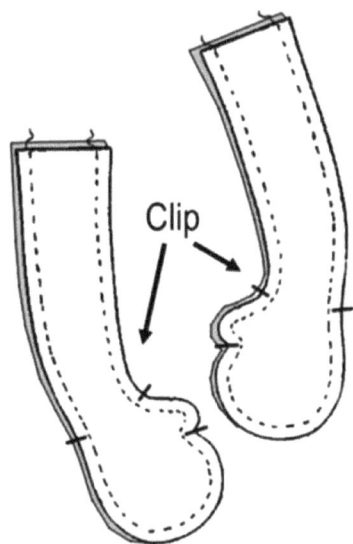

ARMS: Right sides together, stitch the arms. Clip curves. Turn right side out.

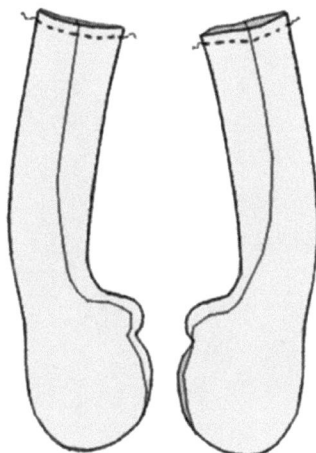

Stuff the arms to about 1 inch from the top. Turn the top edge inside 1/4 inch and pin closed. Hand sew or machine stitch closed.

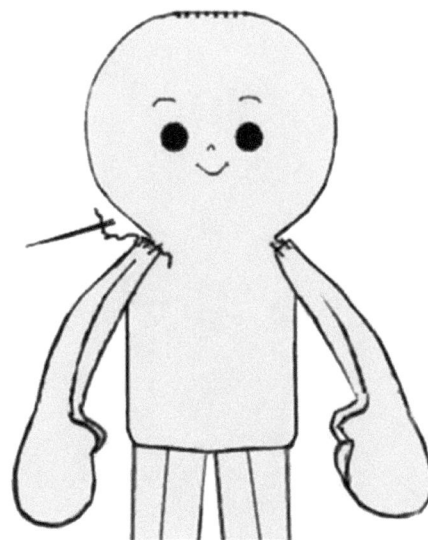

Pin arms to shoulders. Stitch by hand with an overcast stitch.

Making the Hair

Please read all the instructions before starting the hair.

1. For the long hair section of braids, draw a 5-inch line on a piece of copy paper (or material stabilizer) near the middle. This will be where the part on the back of the head will be sewn. On a smaller piece of paper, draw a 5½-inch line down the middle. This will be the seamline of the bangs.

2. For the braids, use a piece of cardboard that measures 18 inches on one side and at least 5 inches on the other side. Wrap the yarn over the 18-inch side 50 times to cover the 5-inch width at the top. For the bangs, use a piece of cardboard 5½ inches by 3 inches. Wrap the yarn around the 3-inch side 45 times so that it stretches across the 5½-inch width.

3. On the long section, place a piece of masking tape about 1 inch down from the top on both sides of the cardboard. This holds the yarn strands together for sewing. Do the same thing for the bangs.

4. Cut the long section and the bangs along the opposite end from the tape. To help control the handling of the long strands, I tie a loose piece of string or yarn about six inches up from the bottom.

Center on
Lines on
Paper

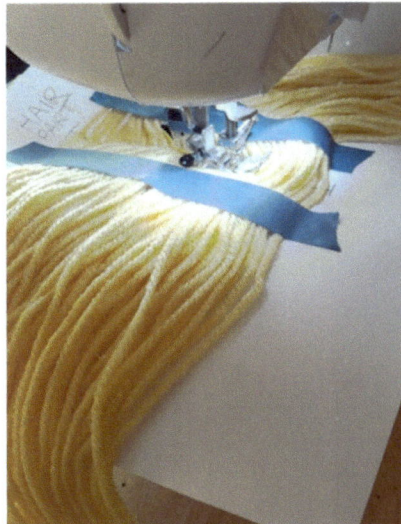

5. Carefully move the braid section from the cardboard and center the tape across the 5-inch line on the paper. The tape should hold it in place on both sides of the paper. Do the same with the bangs.

6. Machine stitch the yarn down the middle between the tape on both yarn pieces. Use a small stitch to create more perforations, which will make the paper easier to remove. Remove the tape and the paper.

7. Center the open seam of the bangs on the top of the doll's head. Pin the seam 1/4 inch in front of the head seam. Using an overstitch, sew the bangs to the doll's head with a thread that matches the yarn.

8. Push the bangs toward the forehead. On the back of the head, center the part between the forehead and neck. Pin in place. Using an overstitch, sew the yarn to the doll's head from the neck to the forehead.

9. On the front of the doll's head, twist one side of the long strands of yarn over the front of the doll's body.

10. Using a long strand of yarn, tightly tie a knot close to the doll's lower cheek. The long strand should blend into the strands of the braid.

11. On one side of the head, separate the strands of yarn into three sections and braid as long as desired.

12. Tie a strand of yarn tightly around the lower section of the braid. Repeat on the other side. Trim the uneven strands at the end of the braid.

Making the Clothes

All seam allowances are 1/4 inch.

Cut out paper pattern pieces and glue/tape Skirt Front to Skirt Back. Cut out fabric.

All edges can be finished by using an overstitch or making a tiny fold inward on the edge of the fabric. I use a pinking shears to cut out my pattern pieces and leave this as my finished edge.

Bloomers

Fold up lower edge of bloomers 1/4 inch. Press.

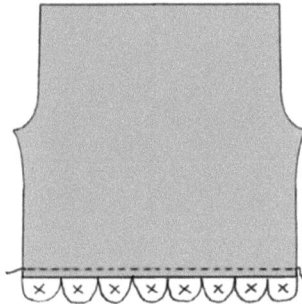

Pin/baste trim to lower edge and stitch. You can attach the trim on either side of the fabric, depending on your preference or on the finished edge of the trim.

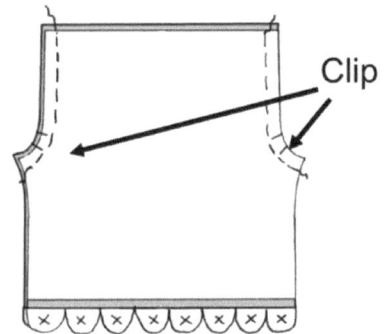

Clip

With right sides together, stitch the crotch seams. Clip curves.

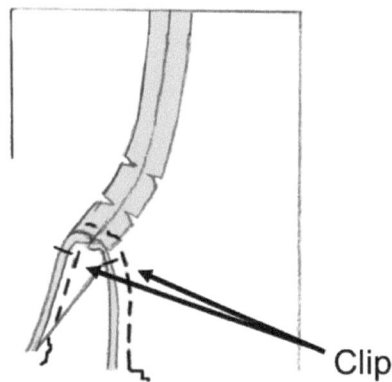

Insert Elastic on Safety Pin

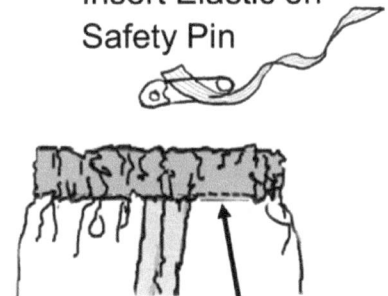

Clip

Right sides together, stitch leg seams from crotch to trim on both sides. Clip curves near crotch. Press seam

Leave open

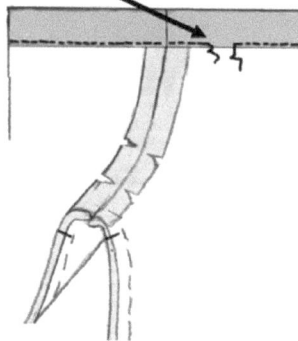

Fold top edge over 1/4 inch then another 1/2 inch to form casing for elastic. Press. Stitch near lower edge. Leave a section open for inserting elastic.

Stitch closed

Cut 9 inches of elastic. Insert into the casing on a safety pin. Push pin through to the other side. Overlap the elastic 1/4 inch. Stitch elastic together securely by hand. By hand or machine, stitch the casing closed.

Top

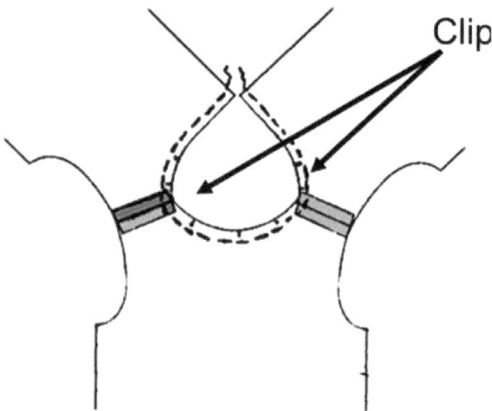

Right bodice sides together, stitch shoulder seams. Press seams open. Stay-stitch around neck to give it stability. Clip curves.

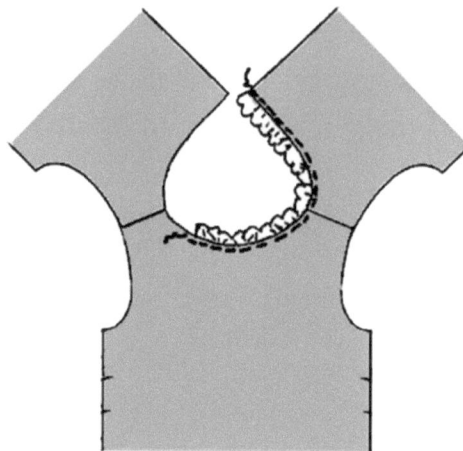

Press neck edge under at stay-stitching. Pin/baste trim to neck and stitch. Trim can be sewn on inside or outside of fabric, depending on preference or on the finished edge of the trim.

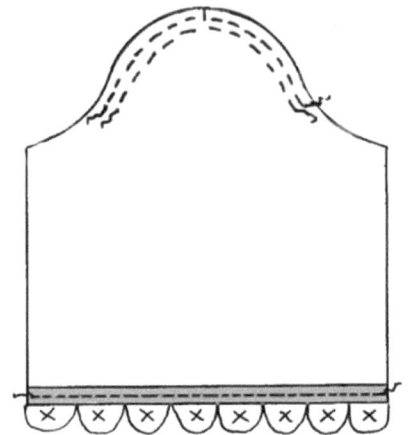

Make two rows of a running stitch at the top of the sleeve for gathering. Press the lower edge under 1/4 inch. Pin/baste trim and stitch.

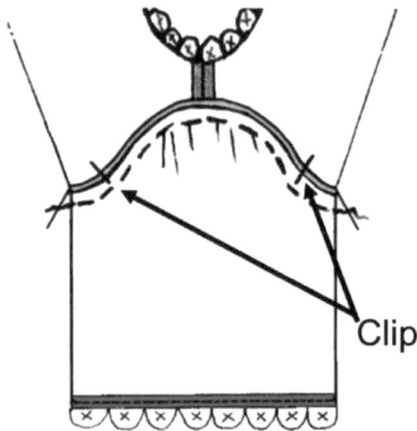

Right sides together, match center of sleeve to the shoulder seam. Pull up gathering threads to fit armhole. Pin/baste sleeve to armhole and stitch. Clip curves.

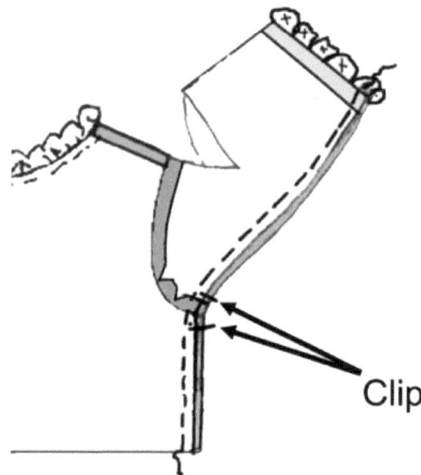

Fold armhole seam toward sleeve. Pin/baste and stitch the underarm seams from the bodice to the end of the sleeve trim. Clip curves where bodice and sleeve meet.

Press lower edge under 1/4 inch, then another 1/4 inch to form hem. Stitch.

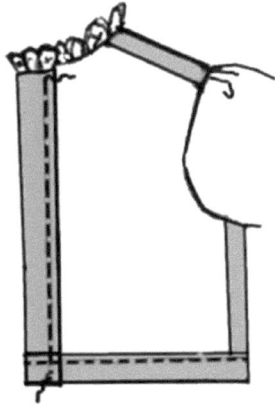

Fold facing over wrong side of bodice. Press and stitch.

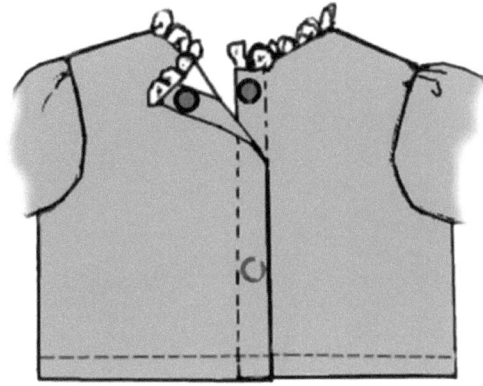

Overlap the left side on top of the right side. Attach snaps to top of bodice and below middle of bodice.

Skirt

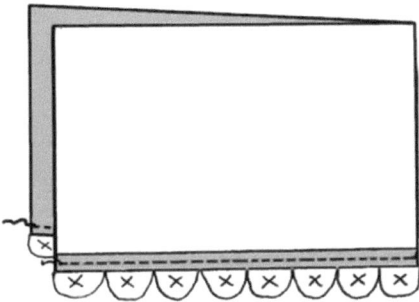

Fold bottom edge under 1/4 inch. Press. Pin/baste trim and stitch.

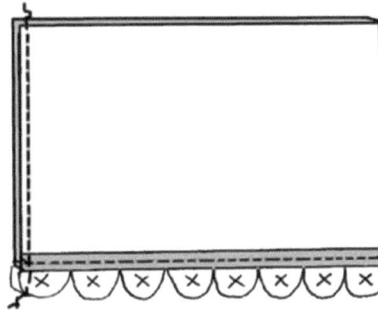

Right sides together, pin and stitch back seam.

Leave open

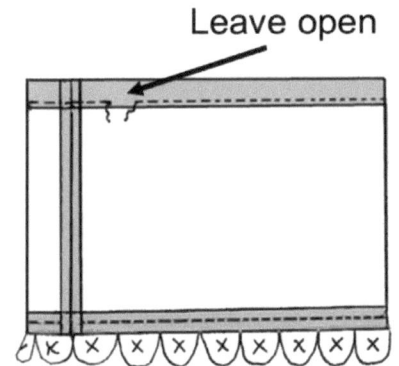

Fold top edge over 1/4 inch, then another 1/2 inch to form casing for elastic. Press and stitch near lower edge. Leave a section open to insert the elastic.

Insert Elastic on Safety Pin

Stitch closed

Cut 9 inches of elastic. Insert into the casing on a safety pin. Push pin through to the other side. Overlap the elastic 1/4 inch and stitch together securely. By hand or machine, stitch the casing closed.

Apron

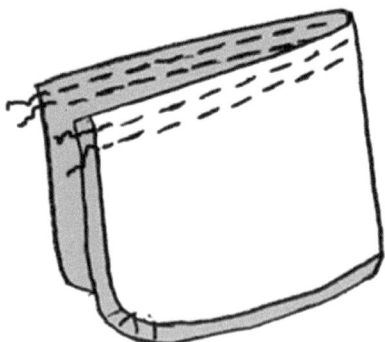

Make two rows of running stitches along upper edge of apron for gathering. Press sides and bottom in 1/4 inch.

Attach trim along sides and bottom of fabric.

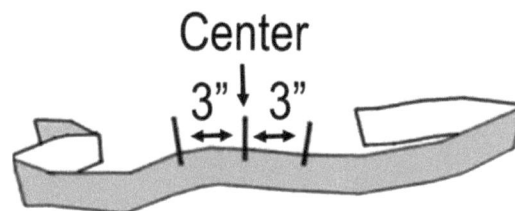

Center
3" 3"

Cut a piece of fabric 32"x2" for waist band and ties. Mark the center of the band and make a mark 3 inches from the center on both sides of the band.

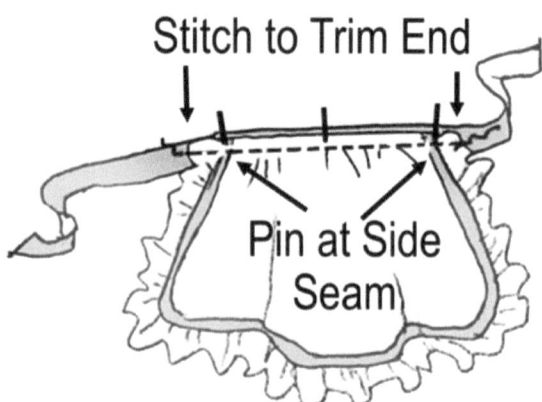

Stitch to Trim End
Pin at Side Seam

Pin center of band to center of apron with right sides together. Pin side seams of apron to 3-inch marks on the band. Pull up the gather threads. Baste and stitch from outer edge of trim to opposite outer edge of trim. Trim should be attached to the band.

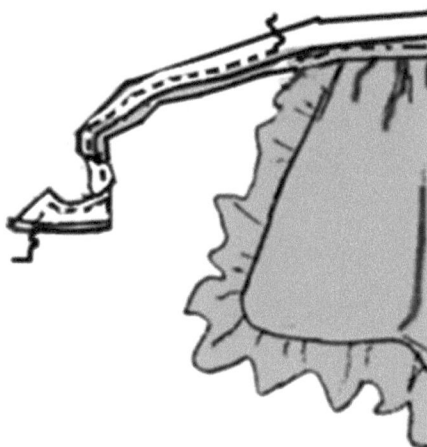

Fold ties on waist band right side to right side toward the front of the apron. Pin and stitch from trim to end of tie on both sides of the apron. Do not catch the trim in the tie.

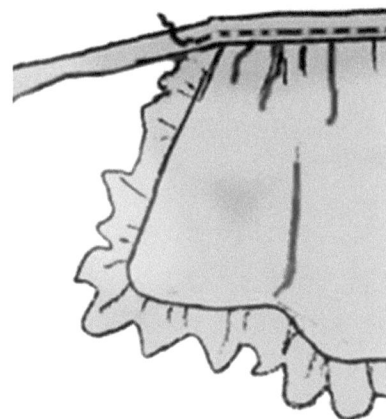

Turn ties right side out, Turn back side of waist band under. Pin and baste. Stitch on front side of waist band close to seam from trim to trim.

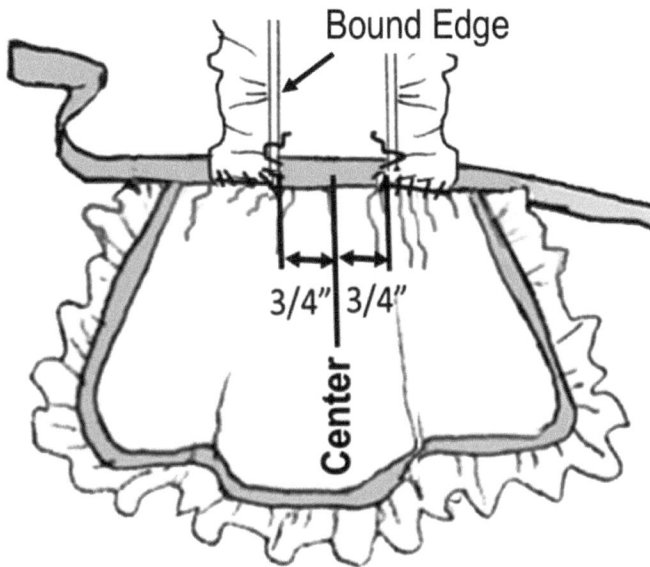

Bound Edge

3/4" 3/4"

Center

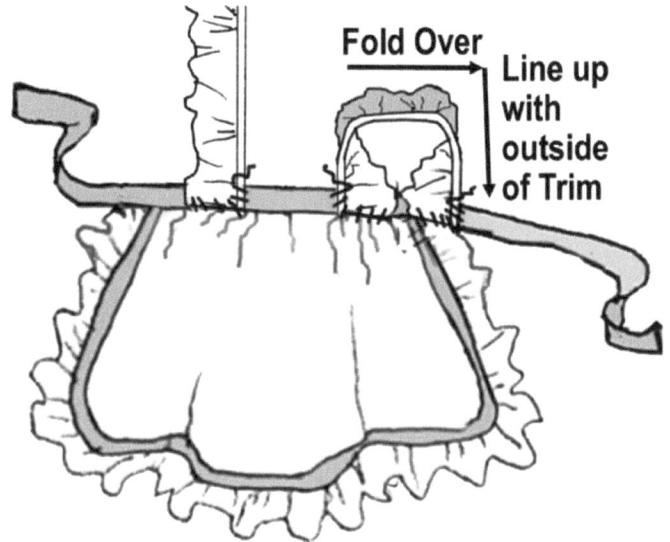

Fold Over → Line up with outside of Trim

For the straps, cut 2 pieces of gathered lace or eyelet 6 inches long on the bound edge. Find the center front of the apron waist band. Line up the strap's bound edge 3/4 inches from the center front on both sides. Fold the strap under 1/4 inch toward the waist band and pin in place. Using an overcast stitch, sew along waist seam and up the bound edge.

Fold the strap so that the bound edge lines up with the outside edge of the apron trim. Make sure the strap is facing the waist band like the previously sewn end. (See diagram above.) Fold the strap under 1/4 inch and pin in place. Use an overstitch to attach to the waist band on the waist seam and up the bound edge.

Hair Bows

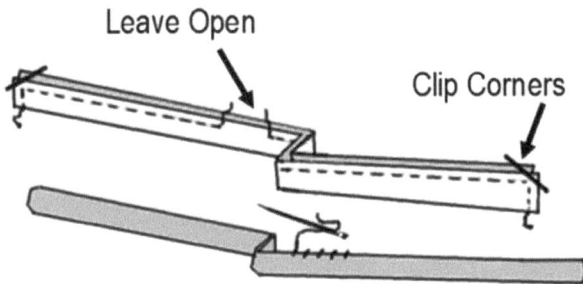

Leave Open

Clip Corners

For hair bows, cut two pieces of fabric 20"x1½". Fold the fabric in half longwise. Pin and stitch, starting from each end and leaving about a 1-inch opening near the middle. Clip corners and turn right side out. Close the open section with an overcast stitch.

Shoes

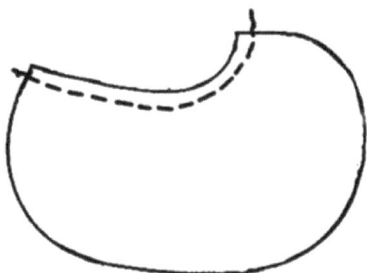

On each shoe piece, stay-stitch along top edge for stability.

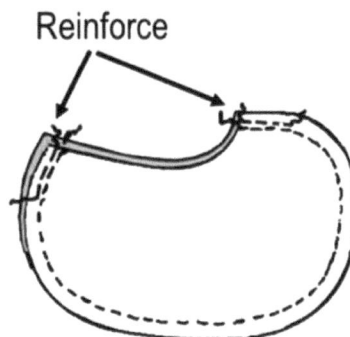

Reinforce

With right sides together, stitch from toe to back of heel. Reinforce beginning and ending with extra stitches for stability.

Patterns
For
Doll and Clothing

Patterns can be cut out or traced.

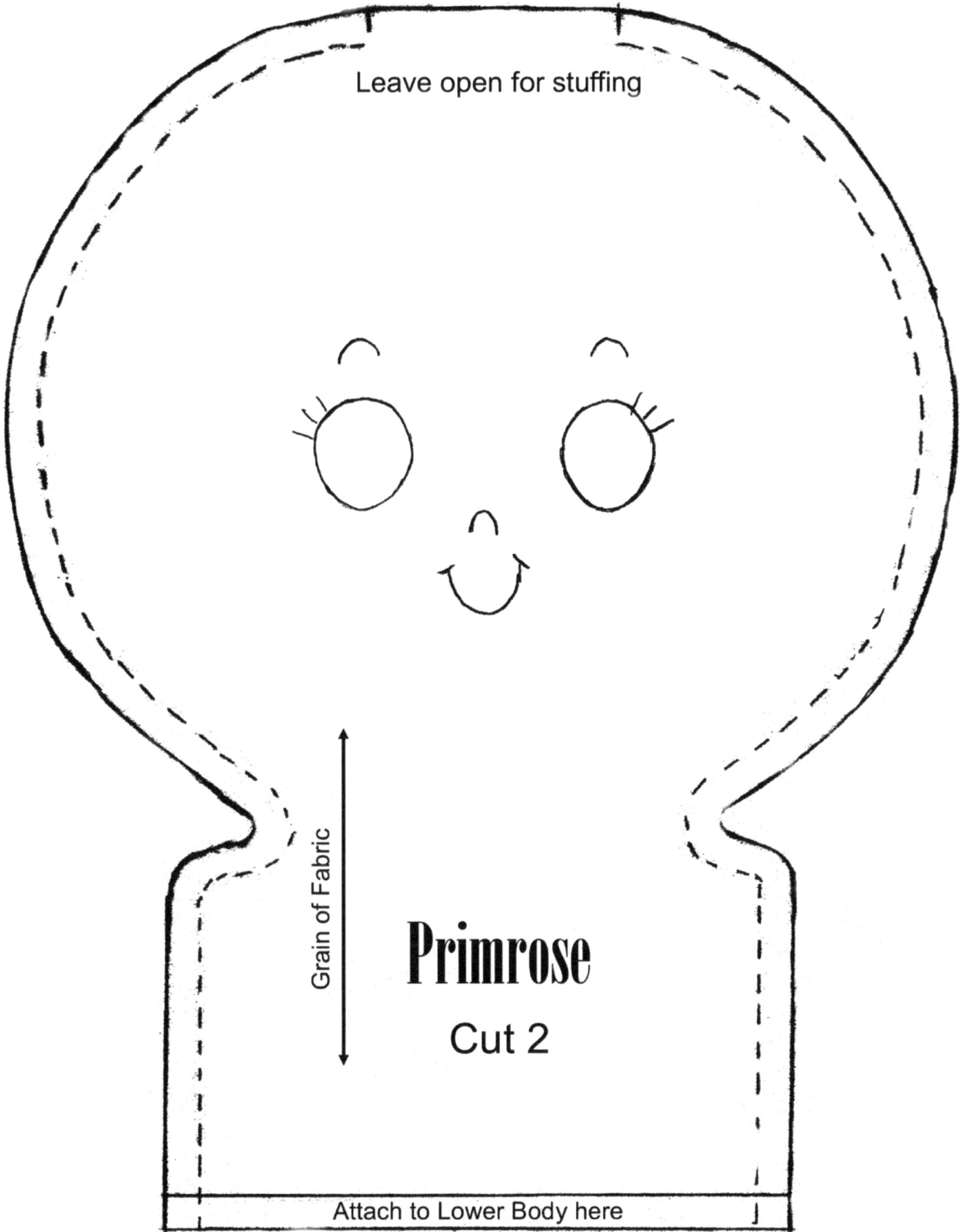

Leave open for stuffing

Grain of Fabric

Primrose

Cut 2

Attach to Lower Body here

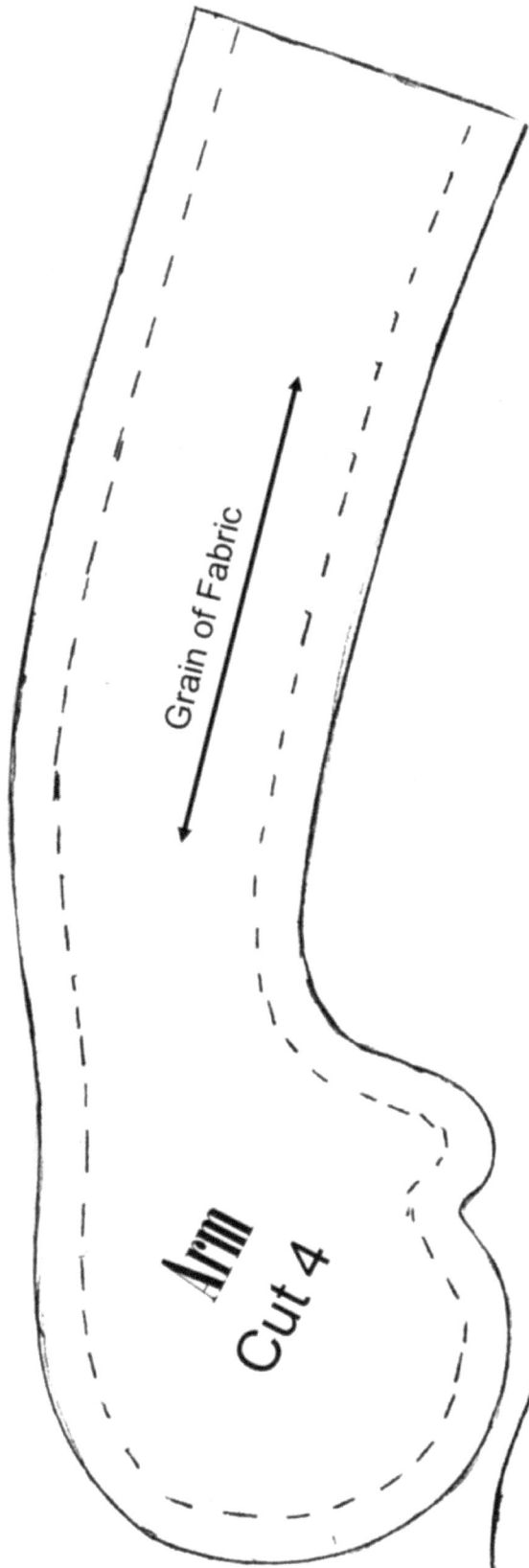

Grain of Fabric

Arm

Cut 4

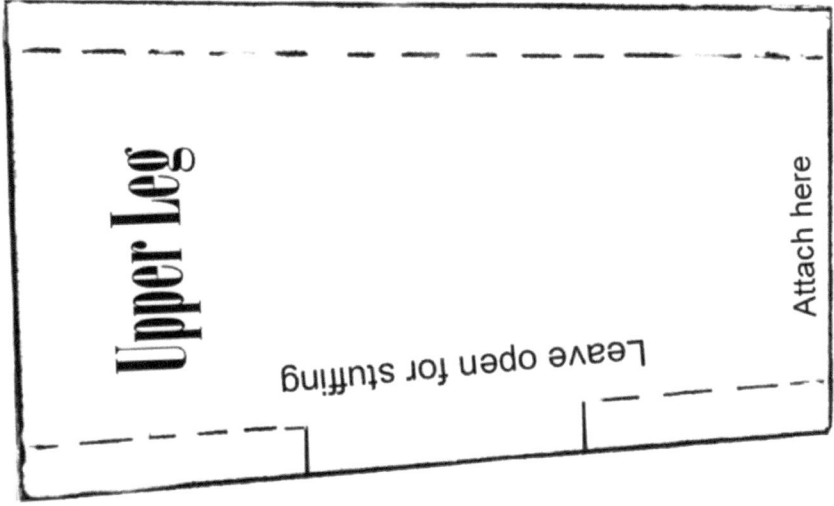

Upper Leg

Attach here

Leave open for stuffing

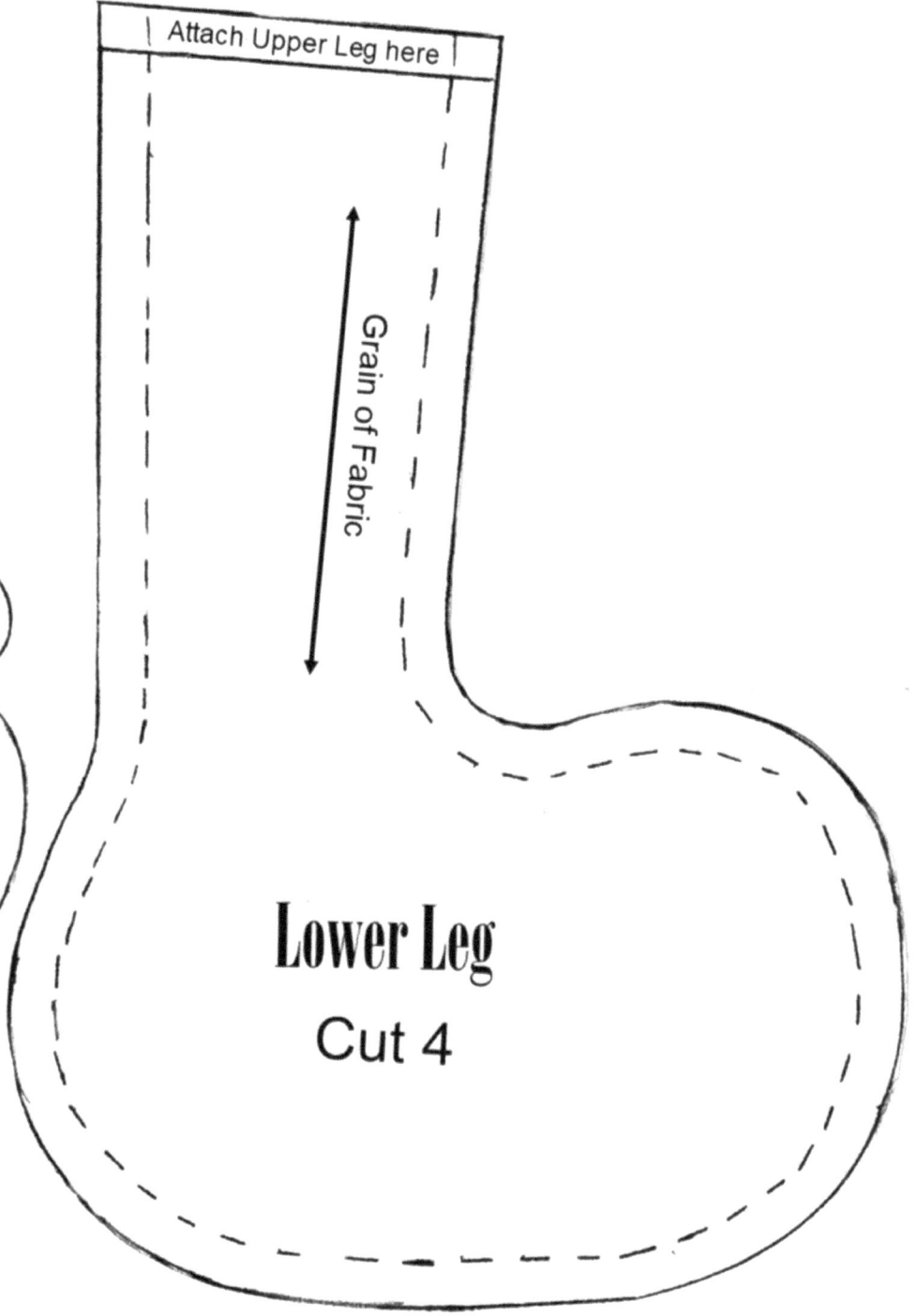

Attach Upper Leg here

Grain of Fabric

Lower Leg

Cut 4

Attach to Upper Body here

Lower Body

Cut 2

Center Line

Primrose

Apron

Gather

Cut 1 on Fold

Add Trim here

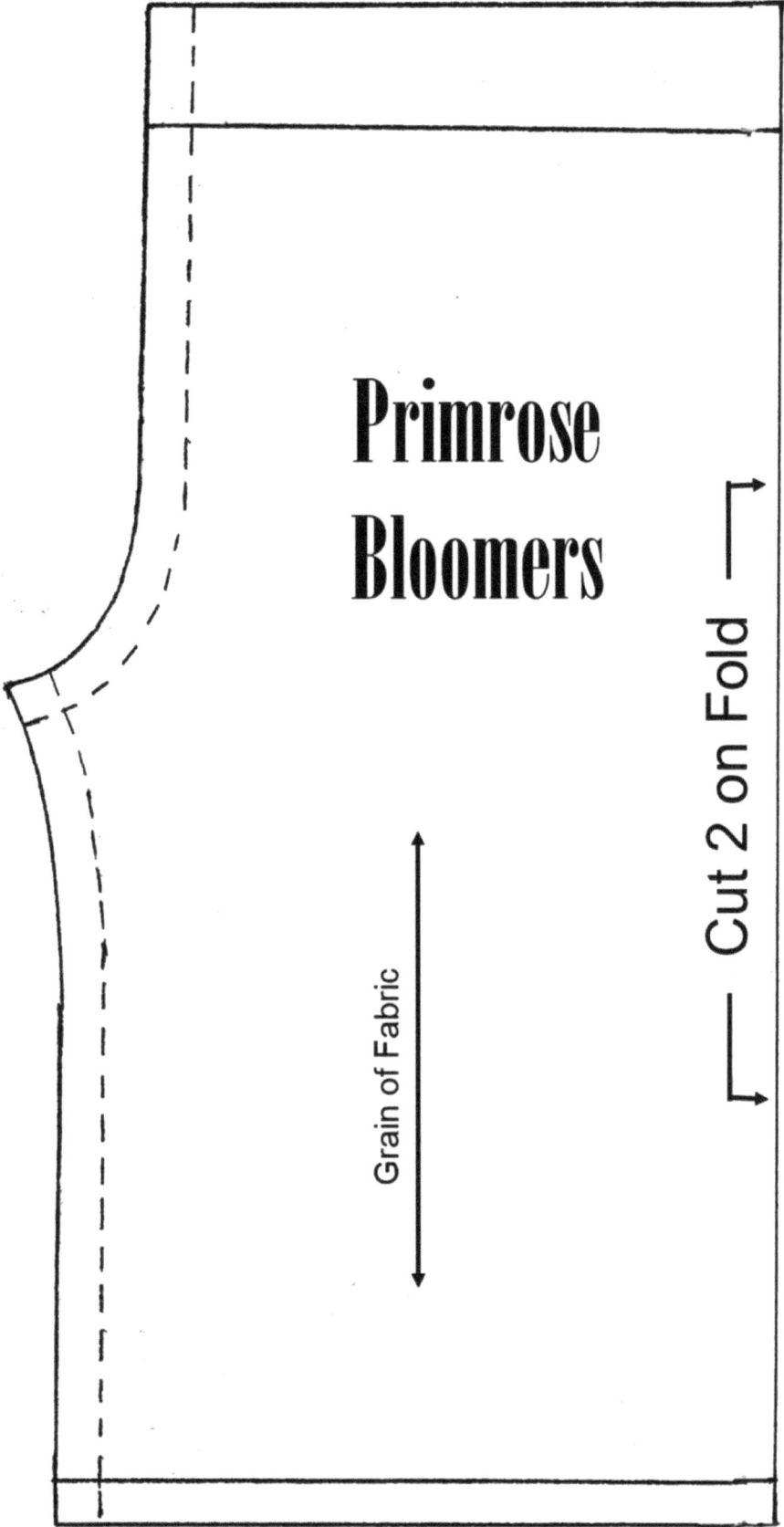

Primrose
Bloomers

Grain of Fabric

Cut 2 on Fold

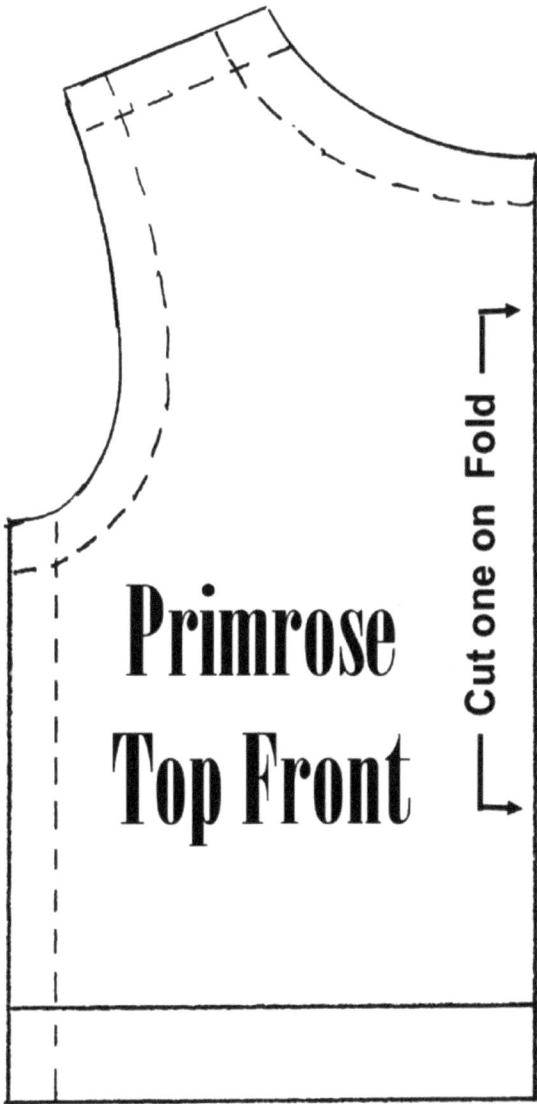

Primrose
Top Front

Cut one on Fold

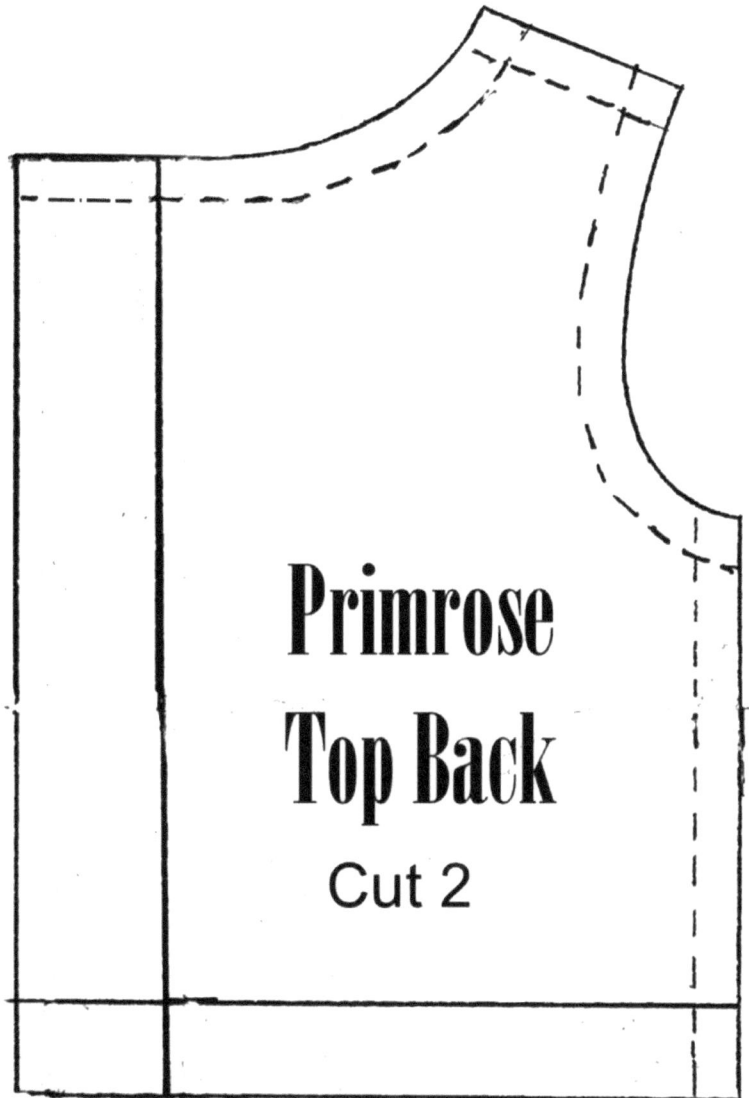

Primrose
Top Back

Cut 2

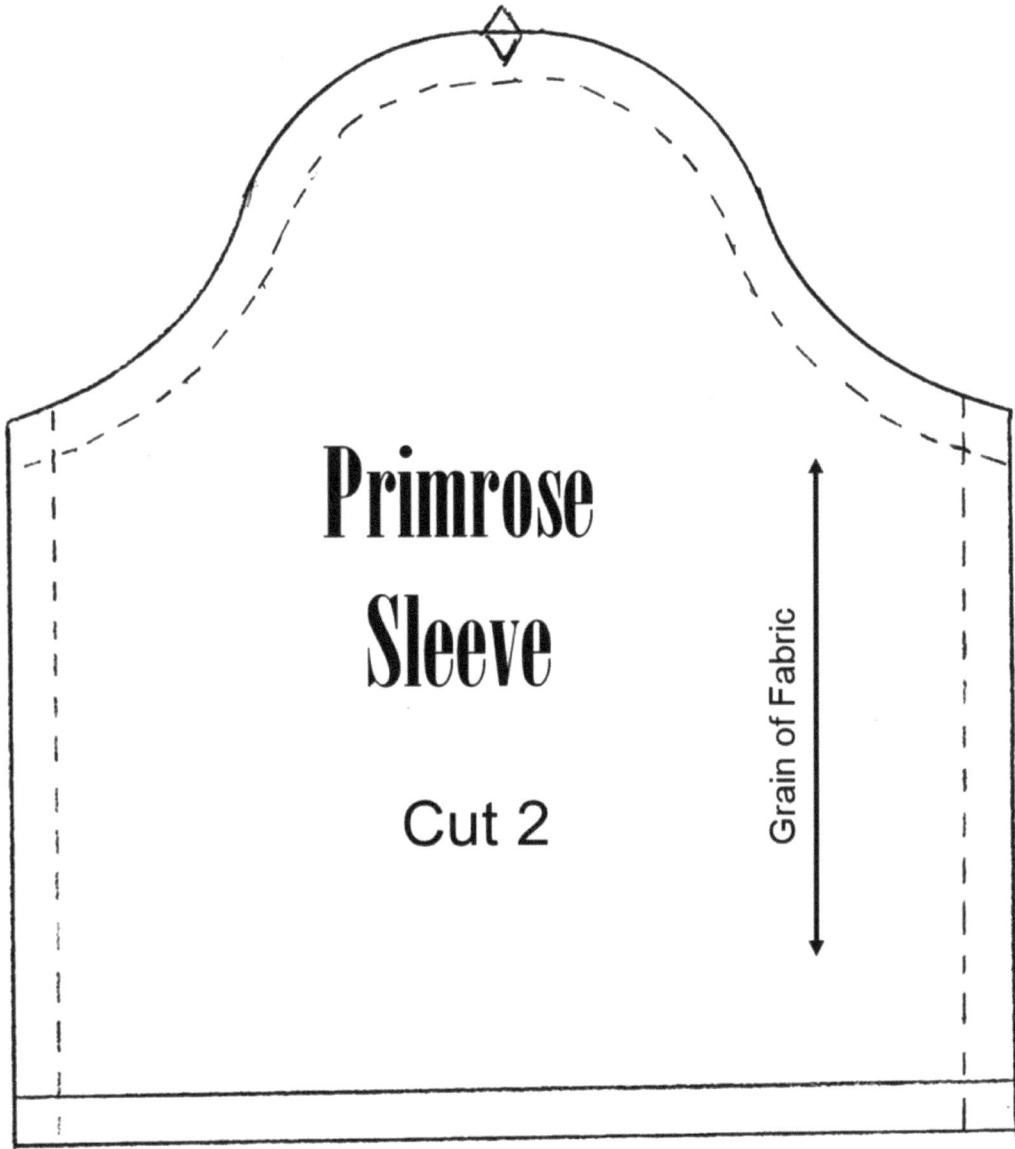

**Primrose
Sleeve**

Cut 2

Grain of Fabric

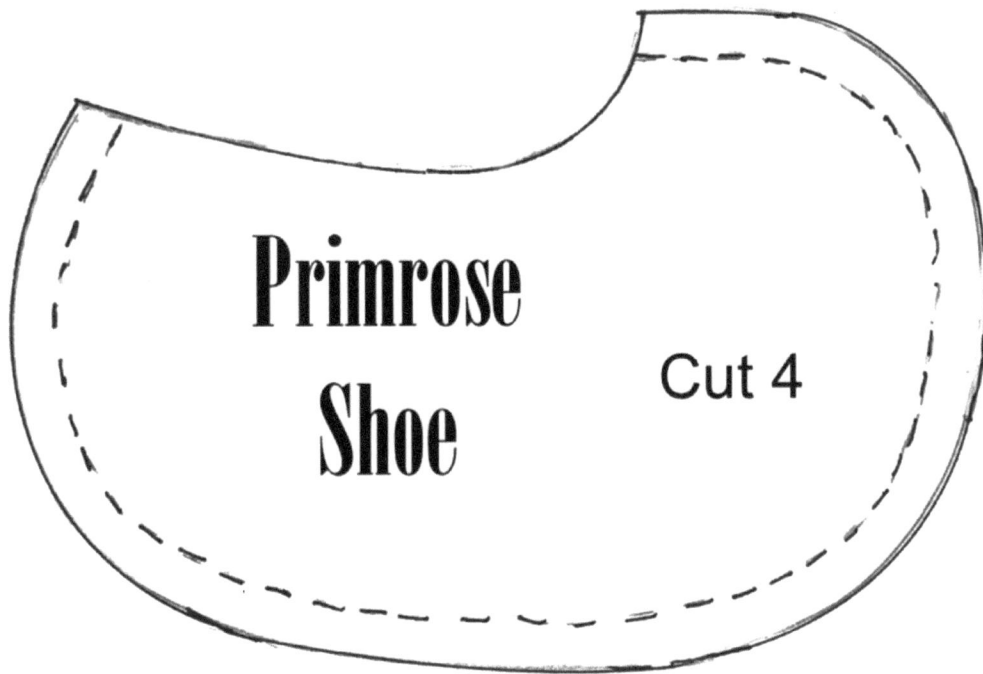

**Primrose
Shoe**

Cut 4

Fold for Casing for Waist Elastic

Primrose
Skirt Front

Attach to Skirt Back here

Cut 1 on Fold

Add Trim here

Primrose
Skirt Back

Back Seam

Attach to Skirt Front here

www.ingramcontent.com/pod-product-compliance
Lightning Source LLC
Chambersburg PA
CBHW041551040426
42447CB00002B/141